Negotiating Caponata

Carla Scarano D'Antonio

Negotiating Caponata

© Carla Scarano D'Antonio

First edition 2020

ISBN 978-1-913329-22-8

Carla Scarano D'Antonio has asserted her authorship and given her
permission to Dempsey & Windle for these poems to be published here.

Section illustrations by Carla Scarano D'Antonio

Cover picture *Cappuccino in Positano* by Janice Dempsey

Published by Dempsey & Windle
15 Rosetrees
Guildford
Surrey
GU1 2HS
UK
01483 571164
dempseyandwindle.com

British Library Cataloguing-in-Publication Data

A catalogue record for this book is available from the British Library

To my family

Acknowledgements

Thanks are due to the editors of the following magazines where some of these poems have already appeared: *The Blue Nib*, *London Grip*, *South*, *The High Window* and Dempsey & Windle's anthologies *20-20* and *Alternative Truths*. I am also grateful to Dawn Wood for her invaluable feedback and to my daughter Irene for insightful discussions about my poems.

... But when from a long-distant past nothing subsists, after the people are dead, after the things are broken and scattered, taste and smell alone, more fragile but more enduring, more unsubstantial, more persistent, more faithful, remain poised a long time, like souls, remembering, waiting, hoping, amid the ruins of all the rest; and bear unflinchingly, in the tiny and almost impalpable drop of their essence, the vast structure of recollection.

Marcel Proust, *Swann's Way* (1913)

Contents

Pajarita   9

Negotiating Caponata

Negotiating caponata   12
Cooking betrayal   13
Farina Manitoba   14
Parsley   15
Smoothie   16
Special carbonara   17
Mid-winter stew   18
What I was leaving   19
Ants   22
Only a cake   23

My Father's Death

Early flight   26
Your illness   27
Cancer   28
Flying   29
At the hospital   30
Your last words   31
Dispersing your ashes   32

In Touch

Granddad Ciccio and Grandma Orsola   33

Mum during the war   34

Volcano   35

Snake eggs   36

Janet   37

In touch with my daughter in Tokyo   38

Cyclamens for my mother   39

What the world throws at me   40

Walking through the seasons   41

The new house   42

Sailing North   44

About the Author   45

Pajarita

My thoughts are tiny ideograms
inked on wrapping paper,
hidden in the folds of my paper bird.

The valley crease
gives space for self-expression,
cradles dreams.
Quarter folds form a thick square,
the plan of a castle keep
makes me think over
the comfort of familiar doings.

When I open the thin wings
the pinwheel spins fretfully
so I hold one end and refold it in half
reversing the little head.

It points forward now, flimsy
but ready to take off,
its sharp tips balance on my hand.
I'll send it flapping across the ocean
picturing our minds touching
like two hands pressing palms
and wait for you to reshape the bird,
send it back to me.

Negotiating Caponata

Negotiating caponata

First peel and chop potatoes in cubes
cook separately in a frying pan
then add peppers and aubergines in pieces;
salt, tomato passata, one or two tbsp., some water,
simmer for one hour or two. Stir.
The aloofness at times.
They are difficult to digest like peppers
or sour like aubergines,
floating adrift or biting back.
But the cut ingredients finally mash together in the sauce,
sensitive and vulnerable.
The body has no protection
when the light dims.

Cooking betrayal

It seems to matter
I use the hob to warm my milk
not the microwave.
It seems to matter I choose rosemary instead of oregano
over beans soup before adding tomato sauce and macaroni,

that I told you he was hooked by melons and plump tomatoes,
though you couldn't believe it
and carried on cooking your usual brown rice —
one dish only — for dinner,
my sister ducking with her marinated cabbage in olive oil.

I was the idiot,
my pointless cake making and biscuit baking
crumbling along the path, signposting my coming back home,
you camouflaged the fennels in thick white sauce and parmigiano
serving it cold on chopping boards,
it was frightful.

But what can you do now?
The peas are squandered on the kitchen floor mashing under our feet.
Who knows what he thought.
Who knows what you concealed under the lids.

Farina Manitoba

A drop in the map,
wide horizon reaching out of the frame,
the transparencies of water ripple in circles,
waves cresting
and the driftwood encrusting the shore.
This is the land of flour —
farina Manitoba I buy in yellow packets
and mix with polenta flour to make cakes and bread
sinking my hands
where earth and water combine;
malleable mixture of snow and turf,
skies and boulder stones
extending its flavour beyond.

Parsley

The fringed leaves look like shredded shamrocks
packed in plastic bags from the supermarket,
its freshness fades in the fridge
better to let the stem drink in a glass of water
to last longer, give it a chance to survive
before you chop or tear it to pieces
to season fish, mushrooms or boil in ragù;
its flavour warms the evening light
when the shadows grow deep and we sit
our faces over the steaming soup
talking about the day
how did it go, any news?

Smoothie

You choose the sharpest pointed knife
and the ripest fruit
to prepare the evening smoothie,
an end-of-the-dinner summer treat.

The skin yields easily
under the penetrating blade,
the flesh is soft and juicy.
You dissect and carve the fruit pulp
piercing deep
slicing it into the blender
precisely and casually,
watching the sport news.

I feel it like a ritual,
the flesh exposed to the
razor-edged cuttings
disappears into the mixer
and we drink it eagerly.

Special carbonara

Liquor is the secret ingredient
and prosciutto instead of pancetta
sautéing with butter and cream.
The dizziness of the beaten eggs
mixing with black pepper and parmigiano.

You turn linguine over in the frying pan,
the gin steaming,
filling the kitchen with thick vapour
in a bellicose conversation.

Entangling and disentangling pasta
with the server and a fork,
straightening words in plain reason.
The mixture absorbs the different points of view,
makes them appetising,
things connect though distinct
and we savour carbonara together.

Mid-winter stew

You stay, attending to the stew
onions, celery, carrots, mushrooms and potatoes
swimming, simmering,
whispering the end of the day;
the chunks of beef sink in the early darkness.
You stay, listening to echoes of broken sticks
conjuring nightmares in the cauldron.

You stay, the vegetables float in the thick sauce
while the stewing beef melts the knots.
Nightmares have no reason,
only shadows now behind you.

Winter seeps through branches
dead leaves disappeared
leaving past seasons flat, unforgiven.

What I was leaving

2014
In the distracted pale sun
shadows hide,
leaves gather in burning rust and ochre,
streaks mark the skin red:
I love their way of dying.

2015
You can feel it unexpectedly
parking the car at the supermarket
or driving home from work.

Before the weather changes
into mist and dim light,
the trees turn gold and vermillion
purple and burnt sienna.

Now it's there
a few days later it's gone,
like an improbable scenario.

2016
Sumac leaves stand out
in the Carnival glow of outstretched branches
like Indian feathers dancing their rituals,
burning inside.

Red and yellow dilute
shadows I attempt to embrace
three times in vain.

Come back from the dead
luggage of junk
digesting the past.

2017
The street ahead is ruddy red
soft like camel coat
shifting under my feet.

The trees above are giants' cocktail sticks tracing the sky,
gathered by an imaginary hand
in a Picking-Up-Sticks game;
they slip and quiver under my touch
surreptitiously.

I pace the surface with light steps
longing to rewind.

2018
Still glowing the sun in the blue sky
though it's chilly at night.
The full moon is ricotta cheese in a sea of blueberry juice.

Now I cook leek and potato soup,
chick peas with rosemary and garlic
and tiny pasta shells,
or rice with lentils, some drops of olive oil before serving.
Their scent warms the house in reassuring airy blankets;
we walk through it as if it's all we have longed for.

Spoonfuls fill our stomach — we won't starve tonight —
while we watch the news side by side;
the soup mashes in our mouths
tasting of childhood minestrone rich with curved macaroni,
our southern persistence beyond ourselves
pulsing.

Ants

One summer, after digging deep in the rear garden
to pave it,
ants climbed up our French window
poking into the living room.
Did we turn their lives upside down?

At first they proceeded in scattered grouping
then ordered queues.
We sealed the French window with silicon,
washed the floor with bleach,
sprayed vinegar and water,
added essential oils, lemon juice, baking soda,
as prescribed.
They came back every night,
every day, a relentless army of black things,
silent invaders,
reclaiming our space.
They reached the kitchen in due time,
found their way to the shelves and cupboards,
biscuit boxes, sugar jar, flour bags;
the tiniest food remains, crumbs
or juicy drops attracted hundreds.
Growing in confidence
they settled under the floor boards.

We gave up,
bought a bottle of ant killer powder —
fast and effective
lasting up to three months —
sprinkled it round their paths.
They disappeared in a day, of course,
their insignificant bodies dissolving under our feet.

Only a cake

'Nonsense,' she said. 'It's only a cake.'
— *The Edible Woman* by Margaret Atwood

It is in the beating of the yolks plus sugar,
the egg cream where frustration releases
its poisoning stings,
in the whipping of the whites stiff
that soften strained strings.

Drops of vanilla essence perfume the substance;
the cup brims with impalpable flour
and sunny butter froths under the wooden spoon
dulling the blobs and bubbles.

The mixture is alive,
grows in the heat of the oven,
a spongy edible thing
sweet and tender,
then cut and shaped in a lady-like cake:
cochineal lips, piped cream for hair
and glossy hot pink dress.
The top is lucid with glaze and sprinkles,
delicious.

My Father's Death

Early flight

My stomach is full of air,
plums for breakfast
and a glass of tap water.

The suitcase is heavy with books,
new clothes and parmigiano,
the LRB under my armpit.

Mum is in bed, she had a bad night,
her flabby fingers barely touch my neck.
Dad hugs me, smacks a kiss,
his beard pricks my cheeks.

Empty streets lead to the airport,
ashen sky; the air still fresh
but thickens beneath murky sockets.

I'm leaving to go back home
as light as a butterfly.

Your illness

was sudden and ferocious.
You thought it was an upset stomach
but your body kept retching
bucketfuls of brown liquid
day and night.
A wounded hawk
clutching his branch.
Mum held the tub under your chin
and cleaned the floor on her unsteady knees
forgetting all the past beatings and shame.

Cancer

You cured your liver stones
and high blood pressure,
ancestral relics,
but metastasis spread everywhere
starting from the pancreas —
shamballa beads cast around
invading and growing
deeply-rooting in your belly.
Called to help the sick
you couldn't assist yourself.

Flying

Back and forth
every two weeks
from Gatwick to Fiumicino,
my brain drained by the day-to-day
and the constant urge to be present.
I kept calling, hoping for impossible news,
couldn't restrain my anxiety
hearing your husky voice on the phone.
Surprisingly,
in spite of all the fights,
your blows and my defiance.
We were your most precious stones,
rings bound to your fingers,
you knew we would scatter
into the dangerous world
when you'd gone.

At the hospital

No cure, but the IV made you feel better.
You asked for ice-cream, espresso,
crackers with butter, soup,
hoping your stomach would keep it.
One night they let me stay,
you felt lonely and slept most of the time
in the dim light of the hospital room,
the sounds like bat wings measuring space.
The next morning you thought you'd pulled through,
were back to your old self
planning an operation and cure.
Don't you dare — you said from your deathbed.

Your last words

At home they gave you morphine,
they said a week or two.
Your belly an improbable balloon
under the bed sheet.
For a second, you opened your eyes —
your Roman nose grasping the air —
lifted an arm, tried to speak
(the last advice?
or threats if we transgressed,
take care of mother, possibly,
and always keep the family ties)
but the drug prevailed,
you were down again snoring loudly.
At night the smell of decay became stronger,
I opened the window to let in the mild April air
and waited in bed
listening to the silence of the night,
your body voiceless and still,
only my memory of you alive.

Dispersing your ashes

The Italian flag flaps on the pole of the Ostia shore.
The tin lid eventually opens,
but who is going in, staging your last wishes?
Your self-deprecating will.
Finally, I do. Who else can do it?
The ashes whirl in the wind, unstrained
mix in the roaring waves of the backwash
making it murky.
They splash on my legs
soak my skirt to the waist.
I wonder if they will leave stains,
then shake the urn empty,
the last specks fly and dissolve,
it lasts seconds.
I wish it longer,
more solemn
conclusive in some way.
The sun is setting in a soaring blue.

In Touch

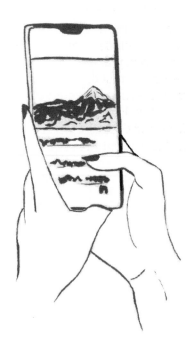

Grandad Ciccio and Grandma Orsola

Sitting serene like ancient Roman statues
grandad Ciccio and grandma Orsola in Merano
with their first baby daughter on their lap.
He in grey uniform and high boots, she in black dress and hat
against a white background.
From the south straight to the northern border in 1920,
their smooth dialect clashed against guttural sounds;
a bag made of silver-net hangs from her gloved hand,
they are close. His arm touches lightly her shoulders,
looks straight, unafraid.
They are close. His arm touches lightly her shoulders,
a bag made of silver-net hangs from her gloved hand;
their smooth dialect clashed against guttural sounds.
From the south straight to the northern border
against a white background.
He in grey uniform and high boots, she in black dress and hat
with their first baby daughter on their lap.
Grandad Ciccio and Grandma Orsola in Merano
sitting serene like ancient Roman statues.

Mum during the war

It was chilly when you left in the morning
with your mother and little sister
to climb up to the woods to collect firewood.
You picked up dead branches, insignificant twigs
piling them up, imagining to build a shelter
that would defy bombs
for your mum and siblings
refugees in Cortona countryside.

By midday you were back
wood and sticks tied up in bundles
balancing on your shoulders
as heavy as stone.
Then off to the market
to sell them for a few cents
your fingers smelling of resin and moss, red-hot.

Volcano

Crickets fill the lap of night,
walls sweat the heat of day.

On the balcony she mumbles,
words bubble up from inside
boiling phrases she couldn't say
to her late husband
(*the bastard who squandered on his tart*)
and to her daughter
(*the bitch who calls me crazy hag*).

She rubs her head with trembling hands,
squints into darkness below:
the shadow of the other man who came last night —
every night —
begs her to join him;
but it's too late,
he's back in America now.

The city sinks into torrid August.
Sounds brood within,
murmurs beneath closed lips.
She is a sealed volcano.

Snake eggs

We played in the garden of the half-built cottage
my cousins and I
digging holes in the sandy ground
looking for snake eggs.
We scooped them with care
and set them on a slab,
then crushed the soft white shell with stones
staring at the yellow core
dripping down like orange juice
thinking about the poison
they would become;
then we trapped lizards with blades of grass,
my older cousin held them by the neck
touched the swinging tail delicately
felt the pulsing of the heart
and let them go.

Janet

You know when your mum marches in
swinging her necklace chain:
she is the boss, the strong black woman
who came to this country and made her way up.
But she doesn't want her child to go too far,
break barriers yes, but not too far.

Oh Janet, your vermillion fingernails wave,
weaving a protective net around your children,
midnight eyes search their rooms for
hidden traps, devious tracks,
looking out beyond your immaculate blouse
and azure skinny jeans.

You know that to survive they need to be topnotch,
or playing dead to let danger pass,
absent when rage blows up,
when the ritual slaughter happens,
when there are no brakes to human brutality
and the sacrifice falls.

Stay at home my child,
with my curry chicken and cornbread
braids of earth and wire.

In touch with my daughter in Tokyo

I would like to have you near me
to touch you now
to be sure we are part
of the same bond of friendship and care —
a family.

But you are far away —
busy busy, engaged with better chances,
confrontation and confusion,
hard work, swift changes.

Photos on the kitchen shelves beam,
heart-warming smile
in a Howl's-moving-castle mauve t-shirt,
your favourite movie,
and Italian red pepper earrings
on the V&A background.

When I feel sentimental, ache ticks
spreading under the ribs;
I send you a smile
with hearts instead of eyes
clapping hands
a dancing lady and a hug
a pumpkin for Halloween or a halo for your name day.

The impersonal networking
warms me up, though infertile,
reminds me of the importance of imperfection
in our infernal autonomy.

Cyclamens for my mother

You were surprised they were blooming in summer
in my English house,
purpurascens from the Mediterranean,
the foliage curling upwards
the flowers downwards.

In your balcony in Rome
they bend their heads
wither in the hot summer
in spite of your watering them
every morning at dawn
with shaking hands.

Bending, bending your head
learning from the cyclamens,
rolling your thoughts secretly
in imaginary leaves
you stack them in piles then incinerate.

The dead are calling you,
I'll hold your hand walking the last steps of the journey.
The cyclamens shrink within the bulb
under soil till the new season comes.

What the world throws at me

she loses the world in her belly
her thighs are fractions of petals
her face is a riot

rain and smoke smile in a window
wood and sea water listen to the civil war
her hair is a rope out of a refugee camp

old and new things burn cautiously
without breaking anything
nothing that matters

she bends the rake the hook and the shadow
ties continents in small colonies
her body marked by the seasons

Walking through the seasons

Autumn

The soup boils:
onions, leek and potatoes
soften and mash.
Comforting taste of fading memories
deepening in the moonlight.

Winter

A web of branches in the bright sky,
sensing wild geese quacking
in arrow shape.
Skeletons of fallen leaves
in the intricacies of broken sticks.

Spring

The sudden melting frost,
buds bulge indecent
in spring thunder.
Loneliness drizzles on the stranger
zigzagging among daffodils.

Summer

The sun gazes through closed blinds,
faded petals scent the heat
while flies drowse.
Lightning surprises the wanderer
in young leaves.

The new house

has unfilled spaces
I measure with my thoughts,
wide windows and verandas
bursting with light,
a white staircase spiralling up,
knots in the honey wooden floor
like dark birthmarks or gigantic ants
I skip by instinct.
The corners are sealed with golden velvet,
the walls are cream.
On the roof the skylights mirror the blue
in trembling reflections.
I lean from the balcony drowsily
looking down at the grey tarmac,
a pool of flames.

Sailing North

We left with cherry trees blossoming,
people arranging polished horns
in a window.
Opposite to south
vegetation grew rusty,
gold, scarlet red
silver grey, brown.
Inhaling thro,
branches torn bare
frozen. North:
thorn, torn, horn
ton, not.

About the author

Carla Scarano D'Antonio lives in Surrey with her family. She has two degrees from La Sapienza, the University of Rome; one is in Foreign Languages and Literature and the other in Italian Language and Literature. She obtained her Master of Arts in Creative Writing at Lancaster University, UK, and has published her creative work in various magazines and reviews.

Alongside Keith Lander, Carla won the first prize in the Dryden Translation Competition 2016 for their translations of Eugenio Montale's poems. She published a poetry pamphlet, *A Winding Road*, in 2011.

She contributes as an Editor at Large to *The Blue Nib* magazine and as a reviewer for *London Grip*, *Write Out Loud*, *South*, *The High Window*, Woking Writers Circle's website and *The Temz* review. She is currently (2020) working on a PhD at the University of Reading, on Margaret Atwood's work.

More information about Carla can be found on her websites: http://carlascarano.blogspot.com/ and http://www.carlascaranod.co.uk/